SARK
SKETCHBOOK

journal of a local artist

Rosanne Guille MA(RCA)

© Rosanne Guille 2004

Published by:

Cat Rock Publications
La Bruyère, Sark
Channel Islands, GY9 0SE
United Kingdom

www.rosanneguille.com

Printed by Bath Press,
Lower Bristol Road,
Bath, BA2 3BL

Published 2004

ISBN 0-9547171-0-4
(Standard Edition)
ISBN 0-9547171-1-2
(Signed Limited Edition)

SARK SKETCHBOOK

journal of a local artist

Rosanne Guille

For my parents Peter and Debbie,
my sister Stephanie
and my grandmother Hazel

Foreword

This little book is so much more than just a sketch book of Sark, it is an environmental journal; a series of 'moments in time' seen through the eyes of a talented and highly observant artist with a feeling for all that surrounds her and with the ability to illustrate what she sees and feels.

Each sketch of a plant, animal or scenery is not only accurate in detail and artistically pleasing, but also gives a wonderful evocation of Sark in all its moods and that indefinable feeling for a particular moment on a particular day.

Rosanne, brought up on Sark (arguably the most beautiful of all the Channel Islands) is captivated by wildlife and natural history and is passionately keen that the natural environment of the island remains as unspoilt as possible.

Nowhere is this more evident than in her paintings where her feel for the environment and attention to detail give her work the quality that has made her so successful.

Michael Beaumont OBE
Seigneur of Sark

La Seigneurie, Sark 2004

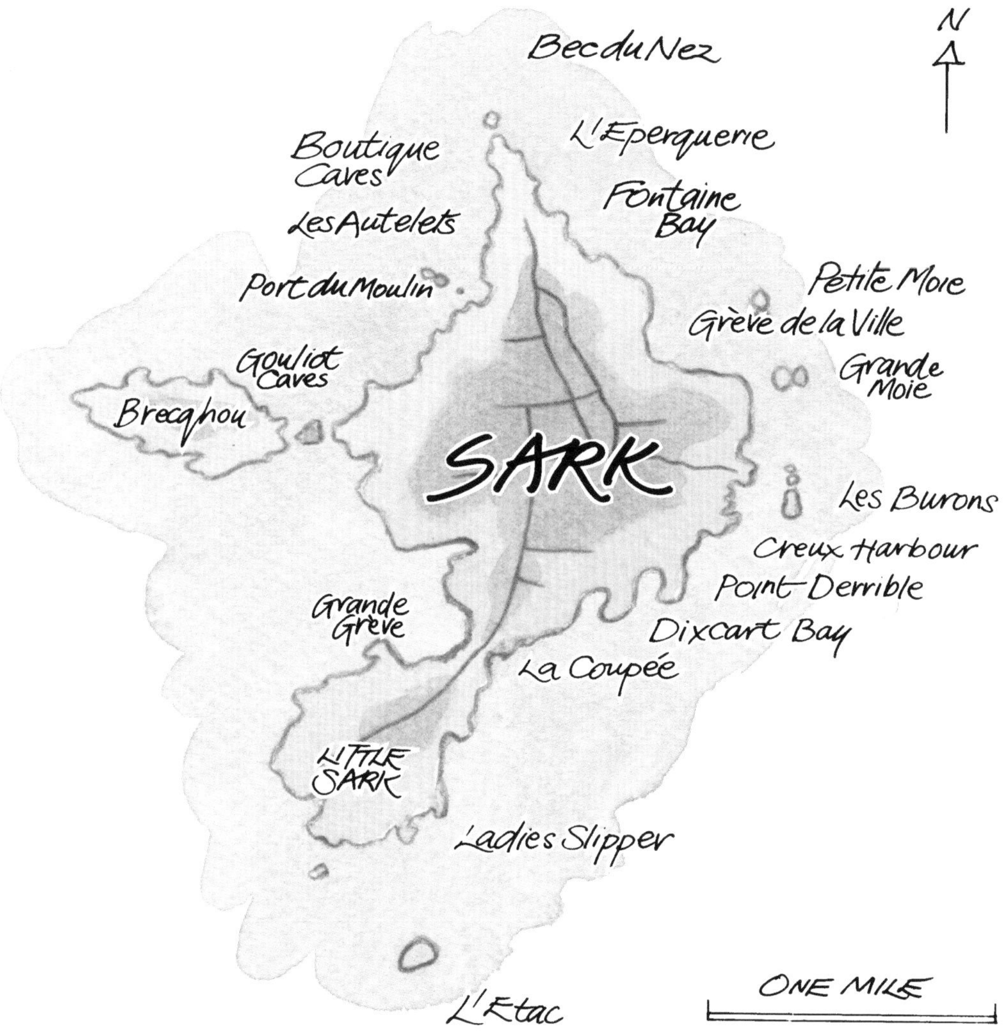
N
Bec du Nez
L'Eperquerie
Boutique Caves
Fontaine Bay
Les Autelets
Petite Moie
Port du Moulin
Grève de la Ville
Gouliot Caves
Grande Moie
Brecqhou
SARK
Les Burons
Creux Harbour
Point Derrible
Grande Grève
Dixcart Bay
La Coupée
LITTLE SARK
Ladies Slipper
ONE MILE
L'Etac

Introduction

I consider myself very lucky to have grown up in such a unique and special place as the island of Sark. From a very early age I began drawing and painting the island and its natural history. I spent time copying the well known local artists and learning the art of watercolour painting.

I began studying at Bournemouth and Poole College of Art and Design in 1992. While on the three year course in Natural History Illustration I had the opportunity to learn the skills required to become a professional illustrator but more importantly to me, getting out of the studio to sketch the wildlife and landscapes in and around Dorset. I spent many memorable days in the New Forest filling sketchbooks and taking subjects back to the studio to paint.

Each holiday was spent at home in Sark painting watercolours of the island to sell; also sketching the scenery and wildlife for my own interest with a view to applying for a Master's Degree course in Natural History Illustration at the Royal College of Art (RCA) in London.

Over the next two years I was fortunate to work with artists equally passionate about wildlife painting in the field. It occurred to me that what I was doing was not just a self-indulgent pastime but could be used to bring to people's attention the importance of protecting our beautiful island and its wildlife for future generations to enjoy.

Working alongside these artists inspired me to paint in a way which would capture the essence of a subject within its unique island environment, rather than just to produce accurate illustrations.

Whilst at the RCA I came across the work of acclaimed wildlife painters such as Lars Jonsson and John Busby and I was awarded a bursary from the Society of Wildlife Artists to attend John Busby's bird-drawing course in Scotland. The course stressed the importance of capturing the spirit of birds through hours of observation in sometimes not very pleasant conditions! The sense of achievement at the end of a day's sketching was very rewarding and gave me the confidence to continue working in this way back home in Sark.

This book is a collection of pencil drawings and watercolours from my sketchbooks produced directly from life over the last few years on Sark. It is not meant as a guide book to the island but as a record of Sark's dramatic coastal scenery and diverse wildlife seen through an artist's eyes. The book takes you on a journey starting at the north and continues clockwise around the island.

Rosanne Guille MA(RCA)

Bec du Nez from the boat

Fairies' Grotto - low tide - bright sun casting strong shadows

the cave behind Fairies' Grotto

Conspicuous black rings

Oak Eggar - 28th February.
I found this caterpillar feeding
on heather. L'Eperquerie is one
of the best places to see the
moths throughout the spring
and summer.

Atlantic Grey Seal – Boutique Caves 31st March

So lucky to have binoculars
and sketch book. I've been
watching the seal for over
4 hours

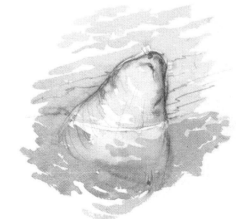

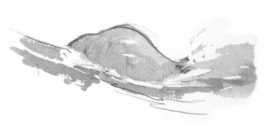

Head back,
showing light coloured
front.

Redwing ~ 12th November

There are quite a few flocks of
Redwing passing through at
the moment. This one is very
underweight, I found it lying
in the road to 'L'Eperquerie'.
Such lovely markings and
Colours.

A really wild day with winds gusting to force 8 from the south west. There's a large flock of gulls sheltering on the water on the east side of L'Eperquerie.

Small Copper

Common Blue

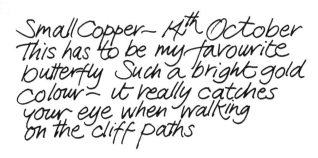

Small Copper ~ 14th October
This has to be my favourite
butterfly Such a bright gold
colour ~ it really catches
your eye when walking
on the cliff paths

Clifftop Fungi – L'Eperquerie 28th December

Tricholomopsis platyphylla

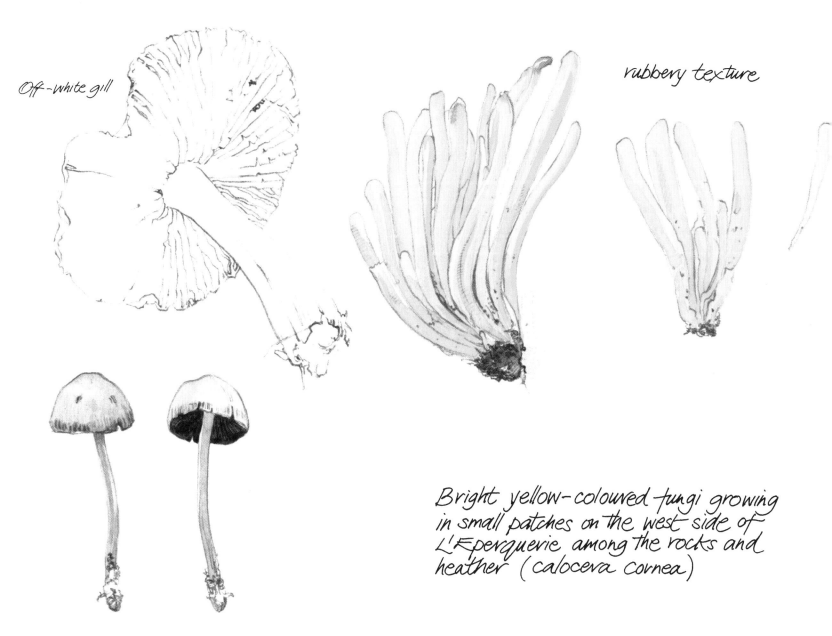

Off-white gill

rubbery texture

Bright yellow-coloured fungi growing
in small patches on the west side of
L'Eperquerie among the rocks and
heather (caloceva cornea)

Black rat (Rattus rattus)

Now one of the rarest mammals in the British Isles - This large rat I often see on cliff paths when out sketching

Ears are larger and more round than brown rat

11th November
Midday, freezing cold north east
force 6. Sea pretty rough in
Fontaine Bay. I can hear a stonechat
in the bracken. It's at times like
this that you wonder if you're the
only person on the island!

Petite Moie, Grande Moie, Les Burons and Noir Pierre from the north

Common Dog Violet

7th December

Candle snuff fungi
in an old dead log

Hart's Tongue Fern
A member of the Spleenwort Family.
The fronds can reach three feet in length.

Maidenhair
Spleenwort

23rd December ~ Grève de la Ville, Alderney on the horizon
A still day, showery with patches of blue sky
Seen a few shags and gulls, also fulmars flying
around the cliffs

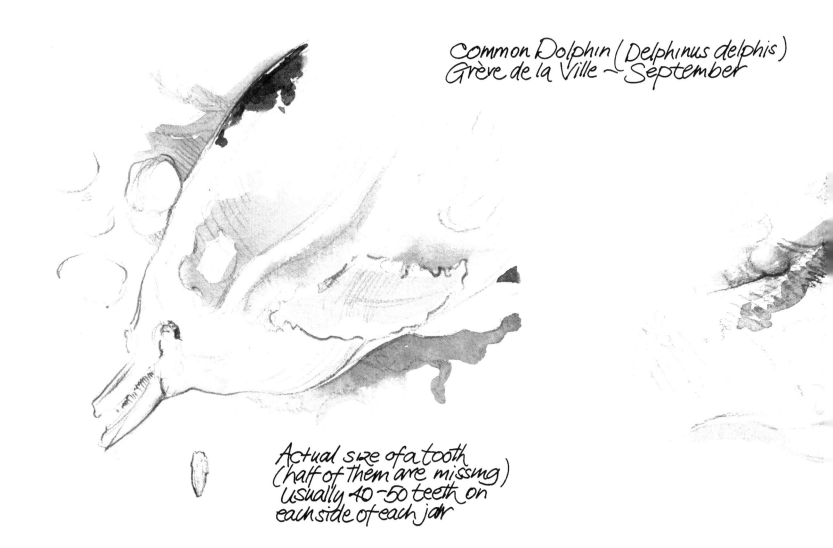

Common Dolphin (Delphinus delphis)
Grève de la Ville ~ September

Actual size of a tooth
(half of them are missing)
usually 40~50 teeth on
each side of each jaw

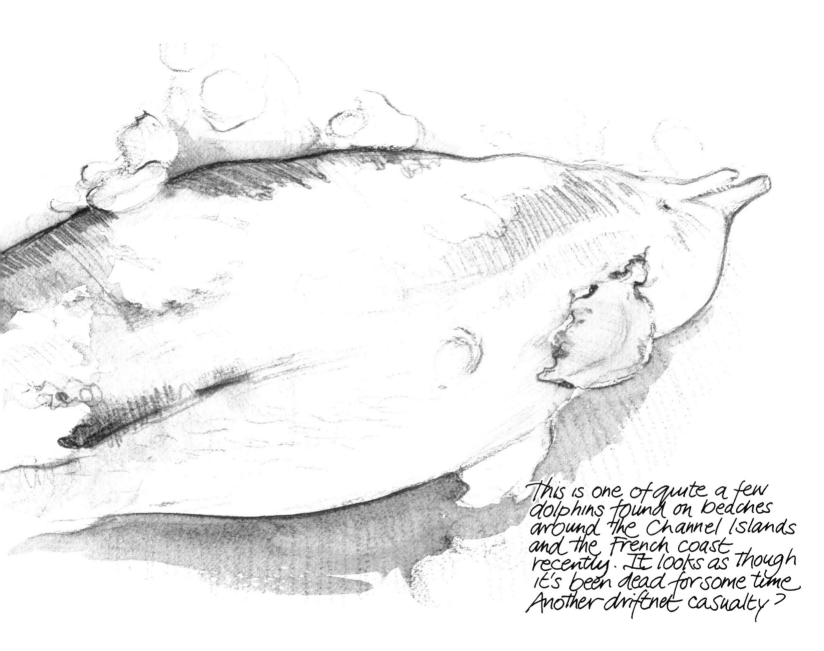

This is one of quite a few
dolphins found on beaches
around the Channel Islands
and the French coast
recently. It looks as though
it's been dead for some time
Another driftnet casualty ?

♀

♂

Peregrines - April

The male just landed near the female and they mated for about a minute. I'm quite a long way from them and am using my telescope. Their yellow feet are showing up well against the dark rock but their bodies are almost the same colour as the granite, so very well camouflaged

Cream Spot Tiger Moth   9th June

This female was sunning herself on a dandelion leaf in the hedge on the path to Greve de la Ville. The moths occur in coastal areas of northern France and southern England and Wales. There's one brood a year, with moths around from May to July.

Female slightly larger than male

January ~
Cold north wind blowing. Fishing boats on their moorings, Maseline Harbour

Grande Moie and Petite Moie from Point Robert

Misty morning, Creux Harbour, 12th March

Juvenile Rabbit

The lesser white-toothed shrew is only found in Sark,
Jersey and around Scilly Isles.
(Crocidura Suaveolens)

This baby hedgehog was
curled-up in the garden – July

Les Burons from
Les Laches headland
low tide

'The Old Lady' (Mormo Maura) July
These large moths are on the wing
in July and August. It has a 2½"
wing span.

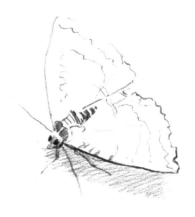

On the wing from dusk –
this species forms one of the favourite
foods of bats the pipistrelle being
the only species of bat on
the island

Point Derrible, 4th November
The morning sun is casting strong
shadows on the sea. Ravens
flying in a strong southerly
wind

Parasol mushrooms – 11th November
I came across this group of 20 or
so mushrooms above Derrible Bay
also several puffballs.

L'Etac and Ladies Slipper from Derrible headland. Calm and misty atmosphere.

Looking towards Little Sark above Dixcart Bay — February.

Left hand side of Dixcart Bay from
the cliff-top. All the birds have been
singing for the last few days and
the wild flowers are just beginning
to show along the cliff paths.
4th February

Great Green Bush Cricket (Tettigonia viridissima)
This female is a juvenile, they can grow up
to 10cm, with antennae measuring the same again
These insects can be heard calling from the
hedges during the Summer months

♀

Pale Tussock Caterpillar (Dasychira Pudibunda)
Found on hop leaves, October

Red tuft at the rear

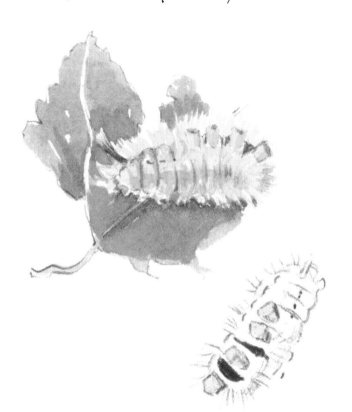

Four yellow
brush-like tufts

Five-spot Burnet (Zygaena trifoli)
found mating in the long grass.
The caterpillars feed on Trefoil and
Vetch which are abundant in this
area — 6th July — field behind
The Avenue.

Lots of bird-life this morning.
These oystercatchers haven't
woken up yet!

Silver mines ~ Little Sark

Little Sark — February.
Lesser Celandines are starting
to emerge in sunny banks by
the roadside, and will continue
flowering until May.

Duval Farm Cottage covered with Passion Fruit—November

Brecqhou, Herm, Jethou and Guernsey from 'La Coupée' April

Grande Grève – rain on the way   14th December

Remains of a Cuckoo Wrasse among the bladder
wrack and driftwood on Grande Grève – 1st January

Fulmars nesting in the cliffs
above Gouliot Caves 8th April

Beadlet Anemones and Breadcrumb
Sponge found in the caves

Jewel Anemones

Milk churns and an old stone trough outside a building at Port à la Jument — November. Everywhere is wet due to the heavy rain over the last couple of days

'Blue stalks' (Lepista nuda) It is an edible late-fruiting fungi, a common species with a fruity taste and smell.

Song Thrush

Wax Caps

Les Autelets from Tintageu ~ January
Flat calm sea, lots of seabird activity,
gulls and oystercatchers calling
constantly. Last night's frost still
on the ground in shady areas, and
even the waterfall to Port du Moulin
has icicles around the edges

A beautifully smooth pebble – washed clean by the tide

`Velvet Horn` seaweed

Quite a lot of marine debris scattered on the beach
The wonderful rocks on this part of the island are such beautiful yellow ochres and rusty reds

Natural Rock Arch – Port du Moulin

Grand Autelet - 24th February
A foggy drizzly day
I've walked around the cliff
path above Port du Moulin
to see if the guillemots have
arrived yet, and there are
at least a hundred on their
usual spot on the ledge of
the north face. The high tide
is surging around the base
of this impressive stack and
the birds are calling constantly
A truly magnificent sight

When one Guillemot lands, the others are very 'loud'! A couple of hours ago I snorkelled around to watch them diving for fish. They are so graceful under water.

The Guillemots egg is
laid on bare rock
and is pear-shaped,
so it rolls in a circle
and not over the
cliff edge.

Guillemots look very awkward on land because they sit on the backs of their legs and shuffle along!

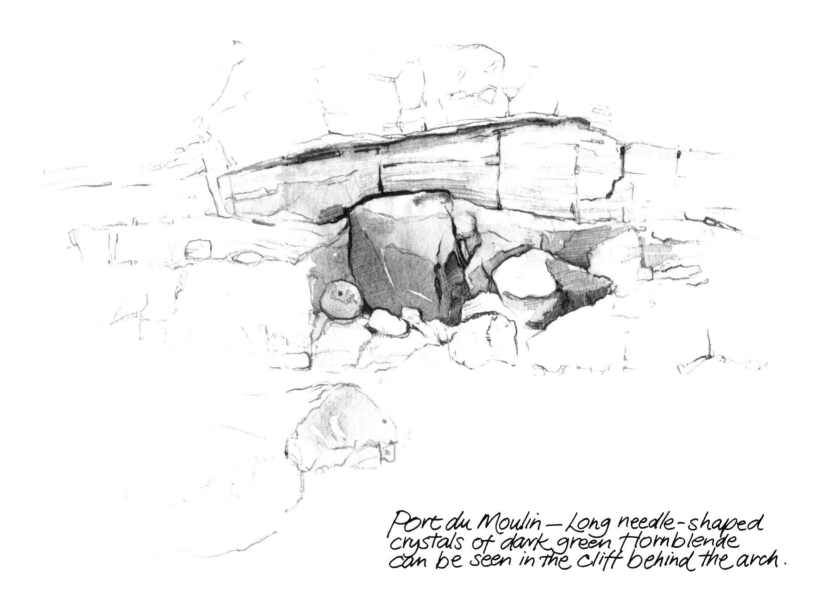

Port du Moulin — Long needle-shaped crystals of dark green Hornblende can be seen in the cliff behind the arch.

Sunset – Brecqhou 18th November

Lesser black-backed gulls starting to pair-up on the grassy slopes around Camel's Head Rocks – 15th April

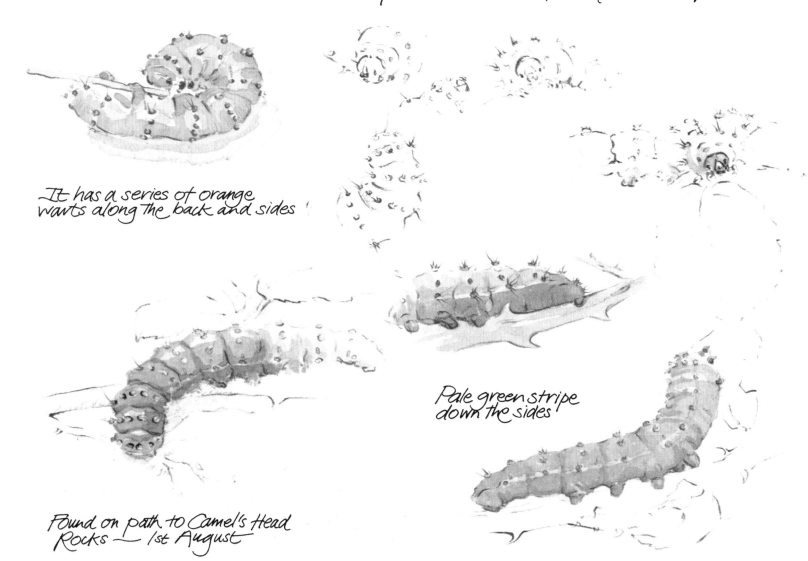

Emperor Moth Caterpillar (Saturnia pavonia)

It has a series of orange warts along the back and sides

Pale green stripe down the sides

Found on path to Camel's Head Rocks — 1st August

Shags waiting patiently for
the right tide to go fishing.

Camel's Head Rocks

Courting Shags — 28th March

Jerky stabbing head movements

Two of the
Seven Sister Rocks

Jersey Tiger Moth
27th August

In the British Isles
this moth is confined
to the Channel Islands
and South Devon.

Legs striped
black and white

Acknowledgements

I would like to thank my family for encouraging my interest in the natural world and for their love and support through my years of training; my good friends, especially Claire and Debbie for sharing my love of Sark and painting, and to the friends of Sark I have met through my gallery.

To John Norris-Wood and other such inspirational tutors for sharing their knowledge and helping me through my homesick moments!

Thanks also to John Syvret for giving his beautiful handwriting to this book and to Stuart Smith without whom I could not have made this project a reality - thank you so much for all your time and effort.

Thank you Michael Beaumont for agreeing to write the Foreword, and 'Woody' Milroy for assisting with the proof-reading.

Lastly, thanks to my canine companion Khan for always sitting in my paintbox and drinking my water!